A TRUE RESCUE STORY

THE ELEPHANT'S
NEW SHOE

written by
Laurel Neme  with a foreword by
Nick Marx
of Wildlife Alliance  illustrated by
Ariel Landy

SCHOLASTIC INC.  NEW YORK

To those who dedicate their lives
to caring for our fellow creatures.
—Laurel Neme

To Mom and Dad, for fostering both my love of
animals and my artistic journey; to Robin, for the
love, encouragement, and colored pencils; and to
all those who work to help animals in need.
—Ariel Landy

Text copyright © 2020 by Laurel Neme
Illustrations copyright © 2020 by Ariel Landy

ISBN 978-1-338-71604-7

This book was typset in Tyke ITC Std and HMS Gilbert.
The illustrations were drawn and colored digitally.
All photos courtesy of Nick Marx.
The publication of this book supports the work of Wildlife Alliance.

10 9 8 7 6 5 4 3   23 24

Printed in the U.S.A.   40
First edition, September 2020

Book design by Sunny Lee

CHHOUK'S NEW SHOE

FOREWORD

When I first saw Chhouk in March 2007 in Mondulkiri, Northeast Cambodia, I wished I were somewhere else. The baby elephant was small, thin, and very badly injured. He could not survive, but I knew I must do all I could to help him.

However, the little elephant I was so sure would die is doing fine thanks to everyone's hard work, a lot of love, and his own fighting spirit. We must not forget that animals have feelings, too. Baby elephants are like children and need love if they are to grow up happy and strong. Please remember this and try to conserve wild animals. They may look a little different, but they are people, too! We should leave them in the forest where they belong, not capture them in snares, put them in cages, or keep them as pets.

We must do all we can to ensure the survival of Chhouk's brothers and sisters and all wild animals everywhere, that make this such a wonderful world!

Nick Marx

WILDLIFE ALLIANCE saves elephants, tigers, gibbons, and other animals in Cambodia by protecting the rain forest and helping communities make a living. The organization rescues animals from the illegal wildlife trade through the Wildlife Rapid Rescue Team. It also supports the Phnom Tamao Wildlife Rescue Center, where injured, traumatized, or orphaned animals like Chhouk receive expert care and attention. Whenever possible, animals are released back into the wild at one of their release stations. When that is not possible, Wildlife Alliance cares for them until the end of their lives. No animal is ever turned away. To learn more visit WildlifeAlliance.org.

Animal rescuer Nick Marx peered at the injured elephant. He and Dr. Thy had been called by a patrol team to inspect a tiny male elephant found wandering alone.

His name was Chhouk.

Nick blinked back tears.
Chhouk was skinny. Scruffy. Scared.
A wire snare had cut off his foot and
his leg was infected.

Nick tiptoed into view. He did not want to startle the infant.

Chhouk flapped his ears. He had been hurt by nasty men before. *Could he trust Nick?*

The baby elephant trumpeted. A warning.
Nick crept closer. *I won't hurt you.*

Chhouk reared up and landed on his bad leg.
His body buckled.

Nick winced. He could feel the pachyderm's pain. To help the orphaned elephant, he knew he would have to prove that he wasn't a danger.

Nick turned back to his team. "Go back to camp," he told them. "I'll stay."

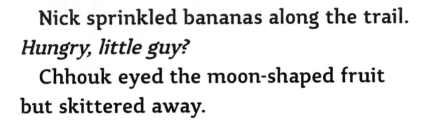

Nick sprinkled bananas along the trail.
Hungry, little guy?
Chhouk eyed the moon-shaped fruit
but skittered away.

At nightfall, Chhouk watched Nick from a distance.
Eventually, both fell asleep under the stars.

The next morning, Nick moved closer to Chhouk.
Banana? Nick offered.

Chhouk inched closer.

And closer.

Slowly and carefully, he placed his hand on Chhouk's head.
At last, the injured elephant snuffled Nick's arm.

The two soon became fast friends.
During the day, they listened to the jungle.
At nighttime, Nick fluffed grass beside his hammock.
Chhouk nestled underneath.

"Bring Chhouk to the rescue center," government officials told Nick. There, he could get the care he needed.

Nick worried Chhouk could hurt himself on the bumpy roads, so they built a special cage and padded it with soft leaves.

On the big day, Dr. Thy sedated Chhouk to make him sleepy and keep the men safe. An anxious elephant can be dangerous.

Nick led Chhouk into the truck and sat beside him.

During the trip, Nick and Chhouk snacked. They stretched. They slept.

Twenty-six hours later, they arrived at the rescue center.

Dr. Thy examined Chhouk's leg. "He's in bad shape."

Nick rubbed Chhouk's trunk. Without a foot, the elephant's back and bones would twist out of shape. The pain would become unbearable. The vets would do what they could. But they could not regrow the missing limb!

Dr. Thy cleaned the wound and removed some bone fragments.

Would Chhouk ever be able to walk again?

Nick and another keeper nursed the elephant round-the-clock. The calf gained weight. His leg started to heal.

But Chhouk was sad. He slept all the time.

Miss your family, little guy? Nick murmured. For an elephant, family is the center of its world.

Chhouk had no mother.

No herd.

No elephant love.

"Lucky, meet Chhouk," Nick said.

Now eight, Lucky had been rescued as an orphan, too. Nick knew she could help.

Lucky nestled Chhouk under her belly. Chhouk snuggled, finally peaceful.

Nick and Lucky started down a lush trail. The tiny calf struggled to follow. His foot hurt and he was tired.

Lucky rumbled encouragement. But Chhouk could not keep up.

Nick frowned. Would Chhouk ever have a normal elephant life?

Nick encouraged Chhouk, but things were looking dismal. Chhouk just wanted to lie down and rest. Walking on three legs was hard!

Chhouk couldn't go on like this forever. He needed a new foot. But was that even possible?

Nick called doctors in Thailand. They had done this for elephants there. But they were too busy.

He called doctors and prosthesis makers throughout Cambodia, but they refused.

Too crazy. Too costly. Too complicated. It was a storm of NOs.

But Nick would not give up.

He begged the Cambodian School of Prosthetics and Orthotics. *Can you help?*

The director agreed. *We'll try.*

Medics measured.
They molded.
They debated and created.

Weeks later, they came back with their first design. It had a soft plastic upper and a car tire sole. Nick examined the false foot. Would Chhouk accept it?

Nick enticed his friend with turnips while doctors slipped on a sock and then the new shoe.

Chhouk nosed it. He took a step.

And another.

He tested. He twirled. Until, at last, he trusted his new foot.

Nick smiled. *He loves it!*

But a few days later, the side split. The plastic ripped.
It could not take the wear and tear of an elephant.
They needed a stronger shoe.

This time, they used a hard plastic.
Nick distracted his pal with turnips while
the team wrenched the boot into place.
The calf trumpeted. *It hurts!*
He cringed. He crashed. He cried.
Get it off!
Nick and the team carefully
approached Chhouk to take it off.

Once again, the team tested different designs.
This time, for a durable shoe, they poured stiff—but flexible—plastic.
For a stay-on shoe, they added belts.
For a comfy shoe, they padded it with foam.
At last, they were ready.

Nick grinned at the new contraption.
Coaxing his buddy with bananas, the
team strapped the shoe on.

Chhouk tiptoed
forward carefully.

He pranced
backward delicately.

He snuggled up to Nick in an elephant thank-you.

Today, Chhouk and Lucky spend their days exploring the forest at the center.

Chhouk is a big boy now. He is still growing and outgrowing his prosthetic.

Every six months, he needs a new shoe. And every time, Nick and the school make one.

More About Elephants

Elephants are the largest land mammals on earth. They live in Africa and Asia.

Asian and African elephants have different ears, tusks, and trunks.

FEMALE ASIAN ELEPHANT

FEMALE AFRICAN ELEPHANT

Asian elephants have smaller ears than African elephants.

Asian elephants have one "finger" on the end of their trunks, while African elephants have two.

Typically, only some male Asian elephants have tusks, while both male and female African elephants have them.

Elephant trunks have over 40,000 muscles. That's more than 60 times the 639 muscles people have in their entire body. It takes years for baby elephants to learn how to control their trunks!

Chhouk holding a tire

TRUUUUUU MMMMPET!

Elephants have big vocabularies. They make many different sounds and combinations of sounds—from deep rumbles to loud cries called trumpets—and scientists are building a dictionary of their meanings.

Elephants eat a lot! They spend up to 18 hours a day looking for food, and can eat 300 pounds or more of trees, bark, leaves, grass, and fruit in a 24-hour period.

Chhouk eating leaves

An elephant's digestive system is not very efficient. Much of what it eats passes right through them and comes out as dung. That spreads seeds and fertilizes soil, which is why elephants are often called "gardeners of the earth."

AUTHOR'S NOTE

Chhouk continues to thrive under the care of Nick Marx, his staff, and Wildlife Alliance at the Phnom Tamao Wildlife Rescue Center, where he has been since 2007. The center is managed by the Cambodian Forestry Administration and is located on 5,600 acres of forest, about an hour from Cambodia's capital of Phnom Penh. There, Nick runs Wildlife Alliance's Wildlife Rescue, Care and Release programs.

Since the center's establishment in 2001, over 72,000 animals—including tigers, sun bears, Siamese crocodiles, pileated gibbons, and more—have been rescued. Those that were sick, orphaned, or habituated to people were taken to the center. Chhouk and Lucky are just two of the roughly 1,200 animals that live there today.

Whenever possible, Nick and his staff release the animals back into the wild. When that's not an option, they care for the animal for the rest of its life. That's the case for Chhouk. Because of his disability, Chhouk could not live in the wild.

Nick often says Chhouk's fighting spirit is what helped him survive. Indeed, his name in Khmer (the language of Cambodia) means lotus. Lotus is a flower that pushes through the mud to blossom—and also is a symbol of triumph over hardship.

Chhouk is now a teenage bull, which can be unpredictable. To keep everybody safe, Nick and the keepers handle him using a protected contact system. Chhouk has received reward-based, positive reinforcement training with food as a reward. That lets Nick and the staff change his shoe, check his leg twice a day, and give him medical treatment without having to sedate him. Chhouk's shoe has two separate parts—a soft flexible inside shoe and a hard durable outside shoe with a car tire on the bottom. Chhouk also wears special socks to prevent chafing.

Thankfully, the Cambodian School of Prosthetics and Orthotics still acts as his "fairy godmother." The school was established to help the thousands of people disabled from Cambodia's decades of war. Now it is helping elephants, too, and building new prosthetics for Chhouk whenever he needs them. So far, Chhouk has had 17 new shoes—but that number will be higher by the time you read this.

Every six months or so, Chhouk needs a new shoe. But every day he reminds us of the possibilities when people like Nick and those at the school care enough to help.

Chhouk in the Sprepok Wilderness

Lucky (left) and Chhouk (right)

Chhouk with Nick and the team

Getting help from the Cambodian School of Prosthetics and Orthotics